CONGRATULATIONS YOU'RE 40

summersdale

CONGRATULATIONS YOU'RE 40

First published 2014 as *40 and Proud of It*

This edition © Summersdale Publishers Ltd, 2016

With text contributed by Vicky Edwards

Summersdale Publishers Ltd
46 West Street
Chichester
West Sussex
PO19 1RP
UK

www.summersdale.com

Printed and bound in the Czech Republic

ISBN: 978-1-84953-902-9

Substantial discounts on bulk quantities of Summersdale books are available to corporations, professional associations and other organisations. For details contact Nicky Douglas by telephone:+44 (0) 1243 756902, fax: +44 (0) 1243 786300 or email: nicky@summersdale.com.

To..

From..

CONTENTS

Life begins
at 40.

W. B. Pitkin

I'm 40 and I feel great. Feel for yourself!

Anonymous

The lovely thing about being 40 is that you can appreciate 25-year-old men more.

Colleen McCullough

As a graduate of
the Zsa Zsa Gabor
School of Creative
mathematics, I
honestly do not
know how old I am.

Erma Bombeck

There was a star danced, and under that was I born.

William Shakespeare

The longer I live the more beautiful life becomes.

Frank Lloyd Wright

Like many women
my age, I am
28 years old.

Mary Schmich

When I passed 40
I dropped pretence,
'cause men like
women who got
some sense.

Maya Angelou

This wine is 40 years old. It certainly doesn't show its age.

Cicero

**Forty is great –
it's the nineteenth
anniversary of
your twenty-first!**

Anonymous

We don't understand
life any better at
40 than at 20, but
we know it and
admit it.

Jules Renard

Every year on your birthday, you get a chance to start new.

Sammy Hagar

Women are most
fascinating between
the ages of 35 and 40...
Since few women ever
pass 40, maximum
fascination can
continue indefinitely.

Christian Dior

It takes a long time
to become young.

Pablo Picasso

At 20 years of age,
the will reigns; at
30, the wit; and at
40, the judgement.

Benjamin Franklin

Women deserve to have more than 12 years between the ages of 28 and 40.

James Thurber

At 15, I had
my mind bent on
learning. At 30, I
stood firm. At 40,
I had no doubts.

Confucius

You're not 40; you're 18 with 22 years' experience.

Anonymous

JUST WHAT I ALWAYS WANTED

Our birthdays are feathers in the broad wings of time.

Jean Paul

When it comes to
staying young, a
mind-lift beats a
facelift any day.

Marty Bucella

I do wish I could
tell you my age but
it's impossible. It
keeps changing all
the time.

Greer Garson

Why is a birthday
cake the only food
you can blow on
and spit on and
everybody rushes to
get a piece?

Bobby Kelton

For my fortieth
I asked her for
a dirty weekend.
She gave me a trip
to the British
Bog Snorkelling
Championships.

Anonymous

**A wise lover values
not so much the gift
of the lover as the
love of the giver.**

Thomas à Kempis

Youth is the gift of nature, but age is a work of art.

Garson Kanin

Yesterday is history. Tomorrow is a mystery. Today is a gift. That's why it is called the present.

Anonymous

Pleas'd to look forward, pleas'd to look behind, And count each birthday with a grateful mind.

Alexander Pope

A hug is the perfect
gift: one size fits
all and nobody
minds if you
exchange it.

Anonymous

Birthdays are nature's way of telling us to eat more cake.

Anonymous

The best birthdays are all those that haven't arrived yet.

Robert Orben

I have everything
I had 20 years ago,
only it's all a little
bit lower.

The ability to laugh, especially at ourselves, keeps the heart light and the mind young.

Anonymous

GRIN AND
BEAR IT

I knew I was
going bald when
it was taking me
longer and longer
to wash my face.

Harry Hill

Age is an issue of mind over matter. If you don't mind, it doesn't matter.

Anonymous

**The first 40 years
of life give us
the text; the next
30 supply the
commentary on it.**

Arthur Schopenhauer

We turn not older with years, but newer every day.

Emily Dickinson

You can't turn
back the clock.
But you can wind
it up again.

Bonnie Prudden

Youth is a circumstance you can't do anything about. The trick is to grow up without getting old.

Frank Lloyd Wright

'Age' is the
acceptance of a
term of years. But
maturity is the
glory of years.

Martha Graham

I believe in loyalty.
When a woman
reaches a certain
age she likes she
should stick to it.

Eva Gabor

It's sad to grow old, but nice to ripen.

Brigitte Bardot

Age is something that doesn't matter, unless you are a cheese.

Luis Buñuel

Stop worrying about the potholes in the road and celebrate the journey!

Anonymous

**Ageing is not
'lost youth' but
a new stage of
opportunity and
strength.**

Betty Friedan

Youth is a
wonderful thing.
What a crime
to waste it on
children.

George Bernard Shaw

**Time has a
wonderful way
of weeding out
the trivial.**

Richard Ben Sapir

Pushing 40?
She's hanging on
for dear life.

Ivy Compton-Burnett

When it comes to
age we're all in
the same boat, only
some of us have
been aboard a
little longer.

Leo Probst

DO A LITTLE DANCE, MAKE A LITTLE LOVE

The older one grows, the more one likes indecency.

Virginia Woolf

I'll keep swivelling my hips until they need replacing.

Tom Jones

There's a kind of confidence that comes when you're in your forties and fifties, and men find that incredibly attractive.

Peggy Northrop

No matter what happens, I'm loud, noisy, earthy and ready for much more living.

Elizabeth Taylor

People dance at any age.

Mikhail Baryshnikov

When our vices desert us, we flatter ourselves that we are deserting our vices.

François de La Rochefoucauld

I am not old
but mellow like
good wine.

Stephen Phillips

The only form of exercise I take is massage.

Truman Capote

I'm limitless as far as age is concerned... as long as he has a driver's licence.

Kim Cattrall on dating younger men

It's sex, not youth, that's wasted on the young.

Janet Harris

Grow old along with me! The best is yet to be.

Robert Browning

Let us celebrate the occasion with wine and sweet words.

Plautus

YOUNG AT HEART

**When choosing
between two evils,
I always like to try
the one I've never
tried before.**

Mae West

**If you obey
all the rules,
you miss all
the fun.**

Katharine Hepburn

I'll grow old physically, but I won't grow old musically.

Cliff Richard

**Men chase golf
balls when they're
too old to chase
anything else.**

Groucho Marx

The more you
praise and celebrate
your life, the more
there is in life
to celebrate.

Oprah Winfrey

I have the body
of an 18-year-old.
I keep it in
the fridge.

Spike Milligan

The older I get, the older old is.

Tom Baker

The best years of a woman's life – the ten years between 39 and 40.

Anonymous

You know you
are getting older
when 'happy hour'
is a nap.

Gray Kristofferson

**Old people aren't
exempt from having
fun and dancing...
and playing.**

Liz Smith

If you give up
smoking, drinking
and loving, you
don't actually live
longer; it just
seems longer.

Clement Freud

It's important to have a twinkle in your wrinkle.

Anonymous

The older a man gets, the farther he had to walk to school as a boy.

Henry Brightman

Some kids in Italy call me 'Mama Jazz'; I thought that was so cute. As long as they don't call me 'Grandma Jazz'.

Ella Fitzgerald

Sometimes when a man recalls the good old days, he's really thinking of his bad young days.

Anonymous

I don't plan to grow
old gracefully.
I plan to have
facelifts until my
ears meet.

Rita Rudner

OLDER AND WISER?

You're only as
young as the last
time you changed
your mind.

Timothy Leary

Be wise
with speed; a
fool at 40 is
a fool indeed.

Edward Young

The best things in life aren't things.

Art Buchwald

Keep true to the dreams of thy youth.

Friedrich von Schiller

None are so old
as those who have
outlived enthusiasm.

Henry David Thoreau

**Old age is like
a plane flying
through a storm.
Once you are
aboard, there is
nothing you can do.**

Golda Meir

Wisdom doesn't
necessarily come
with age. Sometimes
age just shows up
all by itself.

Tom Wilson

A prune is an experienced plum.

John Trattner

There is no
old age. There is,
as there always
was, just you.

Carol Matthau

If I had to live my
life over again, I'd
be a plumber.

Albert Einstein

A man is not old
as long as he is
seeking something.

Jean Rostand

At age 20, we worry
about what others
think of us. At 40,
we don't care what
they think of us.

Ann Landers

As we grow older,
our bodies get
shorter and our
anecdotes longer.

Robert Quillen

If you want a
thing done well,
get a couple of old
broads to do it.

Bette Davis

Everyone is the age of their heart.

Guatemalan proverb

One should never make one's debut in a scandal. One should reserve that to give interest to one's old age.

Oscar Wilde

I look forward to growing old and wise and audacious.

Glenda Jackson

Age is whatever you think it is. You are as old as you think you are.

Muhammad Ali

Age does not
protect you from
love. But love,
to some extent,
protects you
from age.

Jeanne Moreau

Don't let ageing get you down. It's too hard to get back up.

John Wagner

Tomorrow's gone – we'll have tonight!

Dorothy Parker

He who
laughs, lasts!

Mary Pettibone Poole

It's a good idea to
obey all the rules
when you're young
just so you'll have
the strength to
break them when
you're old.

Mark Twain

There are three stages of a man's life: he believes in Santa Claus, he doesn't believe in Santa Claus, he is Santa Claus.

Anonymous

ILLS, PILLS AND TWINGES

I keep fit. Every
morning I do 100
laps of an Olympic-
sized swimming
pool in a small
motor launch.

Peter Cook

As you get older three things happen. The first is your memory goes, and I can't remember the other two...

Norman Wisdom

My mother is no
spring chicken,
although she has got
as many chemicals
in her as one.

Barry Humphries

I don't want a flu jab. I like getting flu. It gives me something else to complain about.

David Letterman

**Middle age is when
you choose your
cereal for the fibre,
not the toy.**

Anonymous

I have a furniture
problem. My chest
has fallen into
my drawers.

Billy Casper

I'd like to learn to ski but I'm worried about my knees... They creak... and I'm afraid they might start an avalanche.

Jonathan Ross

**What most persons
consider as virtue,
after the age of 40
is simply a loss
of energy.**

Voltaire

I go slower as time goes faster.

Mason Cooley

Nothing is more responsible for the good old days than a bad memory.

Franklin Pierce Adams

I hope to have it replaced very soon.

Terry Wogan on people saying that he didn't know the meaning of 'hip'

The older the fiddle, the sweeter the tune.

English proverb

I don't know how
you feel about old
age, but in my case
I didn't even see it
coming. It hit me
from the rear.

Phyllis Diller

Old minds are like old horses; you must exercise them if you wish to keep them in working order.

John Quincy Adams

CHIN UP, CHEST OUT

Anyone who keeps the ability to see beauty never grows old.

Franz Kafka

Professionally, I have no age.

Kathleen Turner

As the arteries grow hard, the heart grows soft.

H. L. Mencken

Inflation is when you pay 15 dollars for the 10-dollar haircut you used to get for 5 dollars when you had hair.

Sam Ewing

Wrinkles are hereditary. Parents get them from their children.

Doris Day

As we grow old,
the beauty steals
inward.

Ralph Waldo Emerson

The spiritual
eyesight improves
as the physical
eyesight declines.

Plato

I'm not denying my age, I'm embellishing my youth.

Tamara Reynolds

I guess I don't so much mind being old, as I mind being fat and old.

Benjamin Franklin

**Age seldom
arrives smoothly
or quickly. It's more
often a succession
of jerks.**

Jean Rhys

**The secret of
staying young is
to live honestly,
eat slowly and lie
about your age.**

Lucille Ball

The most important thing is to grow old gracefully.

Audrey Hepburn

Wrinkles should merely indicate where smiles have been.

Mark Twain

You know you're
getting old when
you can pinch
an inch on your
forehead.

John Mendoza

**Middle age is when
a narrow waist and
a broad mind begin
to change places.**

Anonymous

As you get older,
the pickings get
slimmer, but the
people don't.

Carrie Fisher

People say that age is just a state of mind. I say it's more about the state of your body.

Geoffrey Parfitt

Women are not
forgiven for ageing.
Robert Redford's
lines of distinction
are my old-age
wrinkles.

Jane Fonda

The easiest
way to diminish
the appearance of
wrinkles is to keep
your glasses off
when you look
in the mirror.

Joan Rivers

**The more sand has
escaped from the
hourglass of our life,
the clearer we should
see through it.**

Jean Paul

There is no old age.
There is, as there
always was,
just you.

Carol Matthau

You are never too old to set another goal or to dream a new dream.

C. S. Lewis

If you're interested in
finding out more about our
books, find us on Facebook at
Summersdale Publishers and
follow us on Twitter at
@Summersdale.

www.summersdale.com